PHILIPPE LEGENDRE

KIDS CAN DRAW

Animals of the World

© 1994 Editions Fleurus, Paris.
Published by
Walter Foster Publishing, Inc.
23062 La Cadena Drive
Laguna Hills, CA 92653
ISBN 1-56010-276-4

Attention Parents and Teachers

All children can draw a circle, a square, or a triangle…which means that they can also learn to draw a tiger, kangaroo, or koala! The KIDS CAN DRAW learning method is easy and fun. Children will learn a technique and a vocabulary of shapes that will form the basis for all kinds of drawing.

Pictures are created by combining geometric shapes to form a mass of volumes and surfaces. From this stage, children can give character to their sketches with straight, curved, or broken lines.

With just a few strokes of the pencil, an animal of the world will appear—and with the addition of color, the picture will be real work of art!

The KIDS CAN DRAW method offers a real apprenticeship in technique and a first look at composition, proportion, shapes, and lines. The simplicity of this method ensures that the pleasure of drawing is always the most important factor.

About Philippe Legendre

French painter, engraver, and illustrator, Philippe Legendre also runs a school of art for children aged 6–14 years. Legendre frequently spends time in schools and has developed this method of learning so that all children can discover the artist within themselves.

Helpful Tips

1. Each picture is made up of simple geometric shapes, which are illustrated at the top of the left-hand page. This is called the **Vocabulary of Shapes.** Encourage children to practice drawing each shape before starting their pictures.

2. Suggest children use a pencil to do their sketches. This way, if they don't like a particular shape, they can just erase it and try again.

3. A dotted line indicates that the line should be erased. Have children draw the whole shape and then erase the dotted part of the line.

4. Once children finish their drawings, they can color them with crayons, colored pencils, or felt-tip markers. They may want to go over the lines with a black pencil or pen.

Now let's get started!

VOCABULARY OF SHAPES

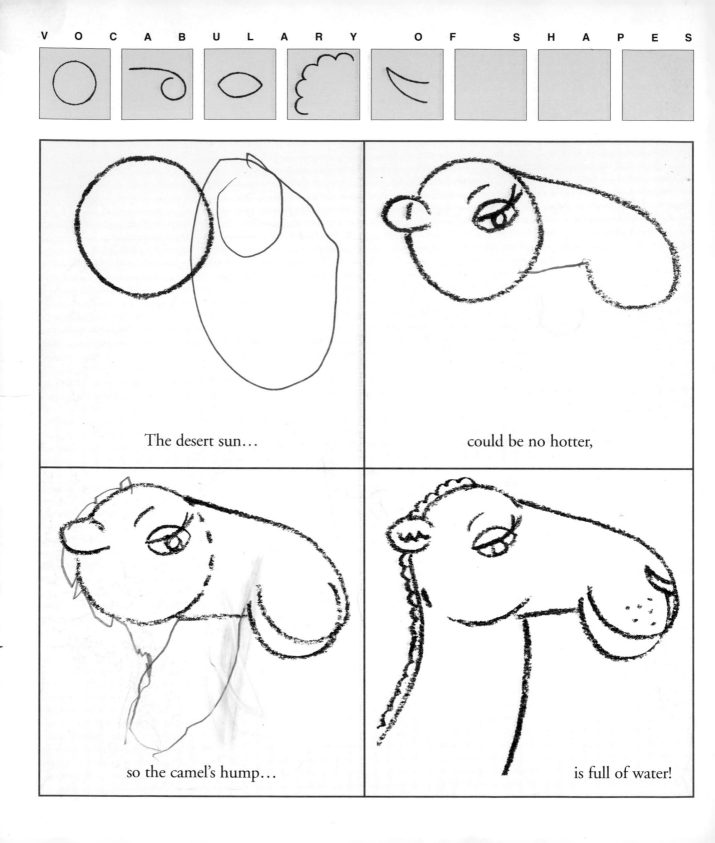

The desert sun…

could be no hotter,

so the camel's hump…

is full of water!

Camel

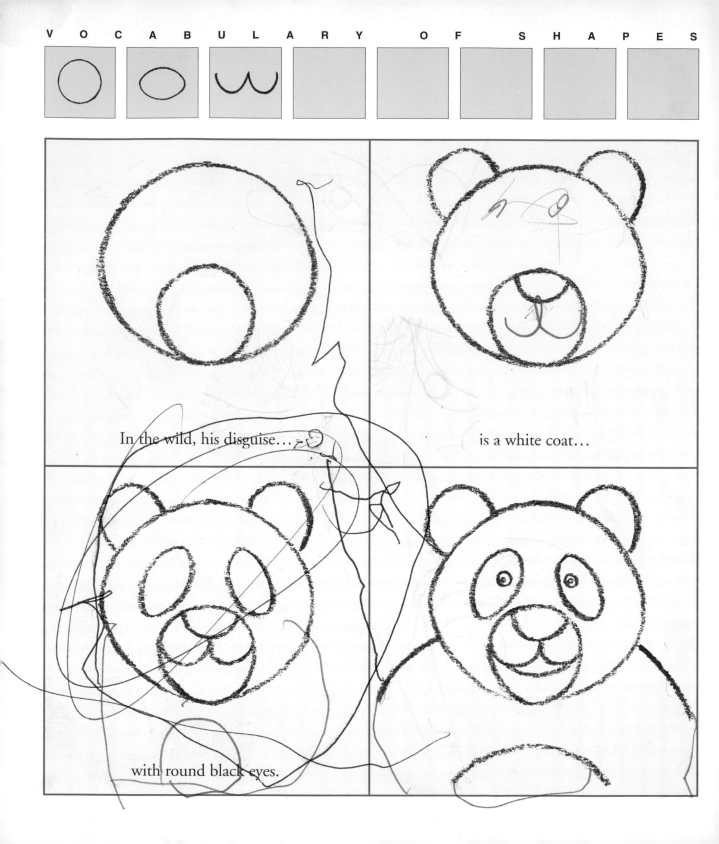

In the wild, his disguise…

is a white coat…

with round black eyes.

Panda

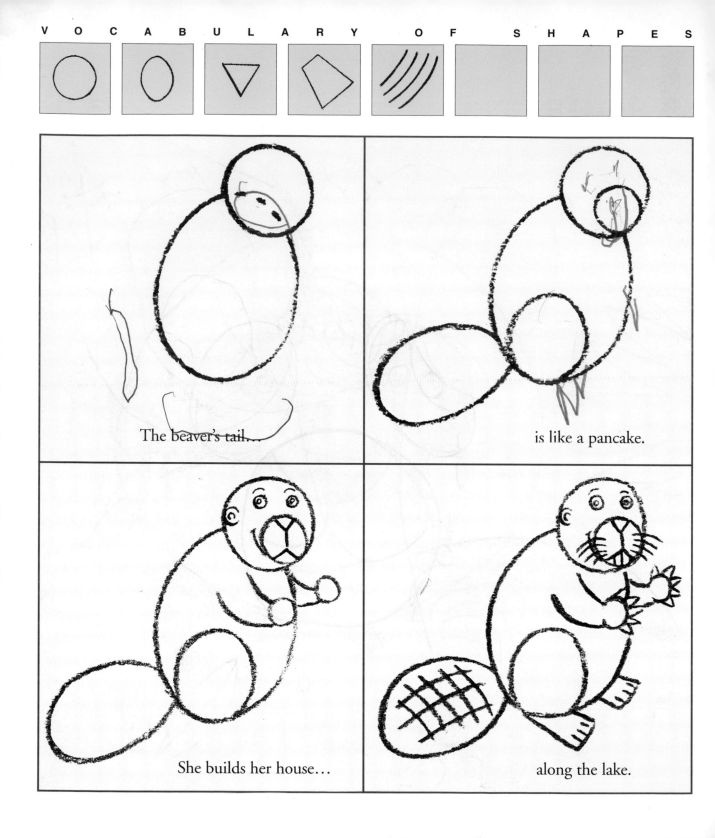

The beaver's tail…

is like a pancake.

She builds her house…

along the lake.

Beaver

The tiger has…

stripes galore.

It can let out a mighty roar.

Tiger

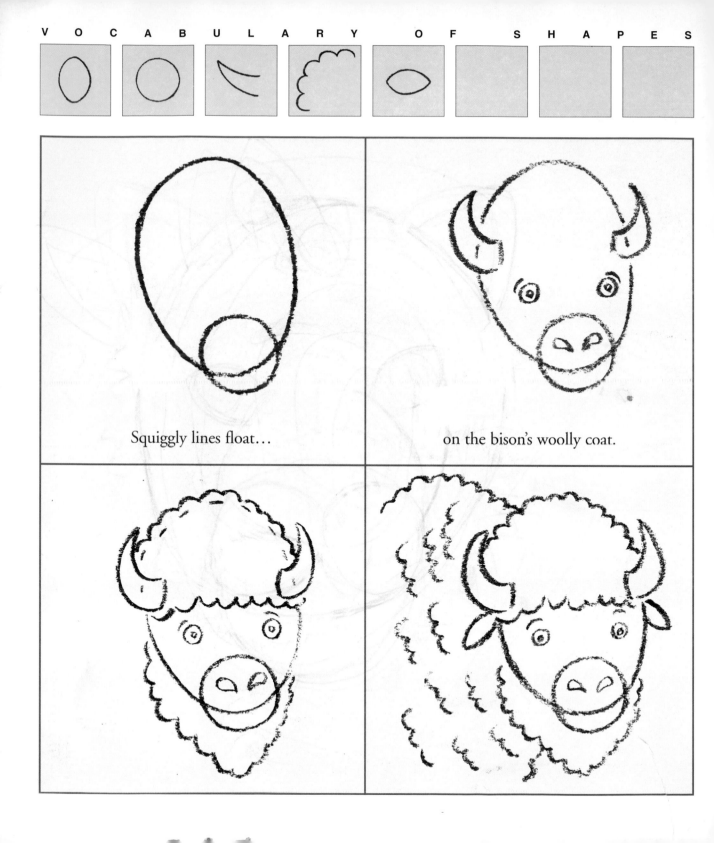

Squiggly lines float…

on the bison's woolly coat.

Bison

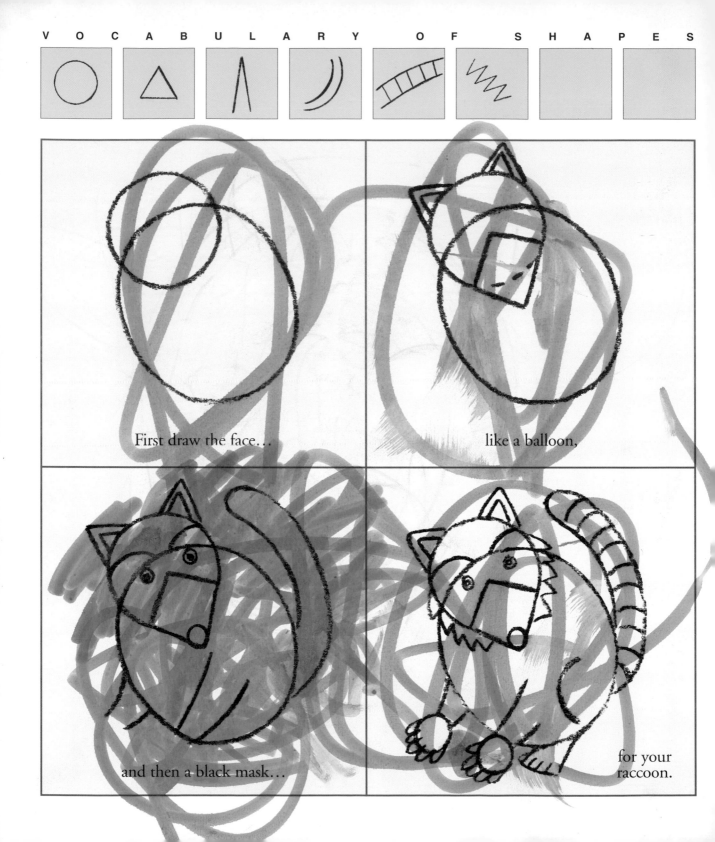

VOCABULARY OF SHAPES

First draw the face...

like a balloon,

and then a black mask...

for your raccoon.

Raccoon

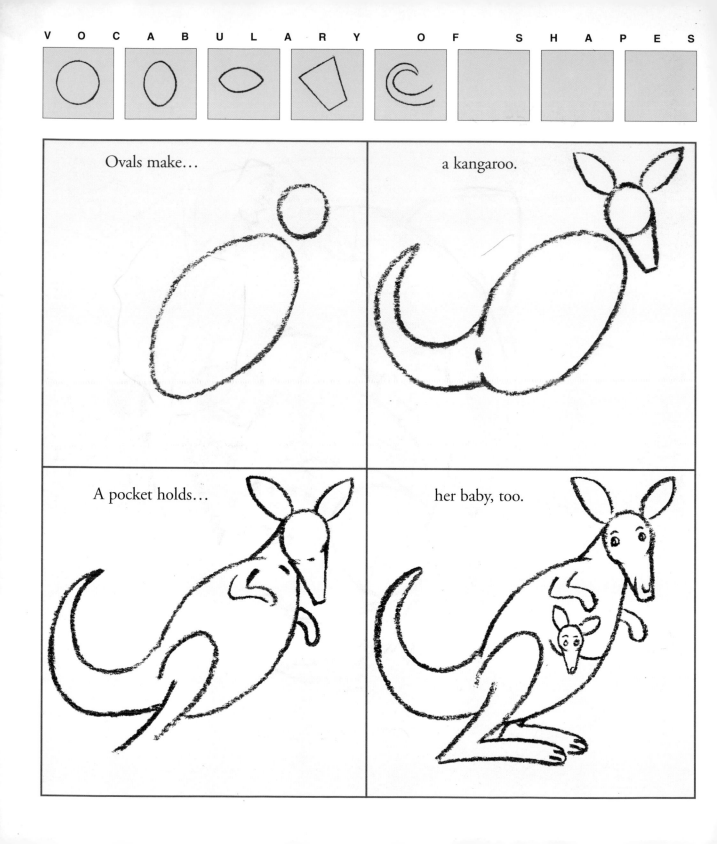

Ovals make…

a kangaroo.

A pocket holds…

her baby, too.

Kangaroo

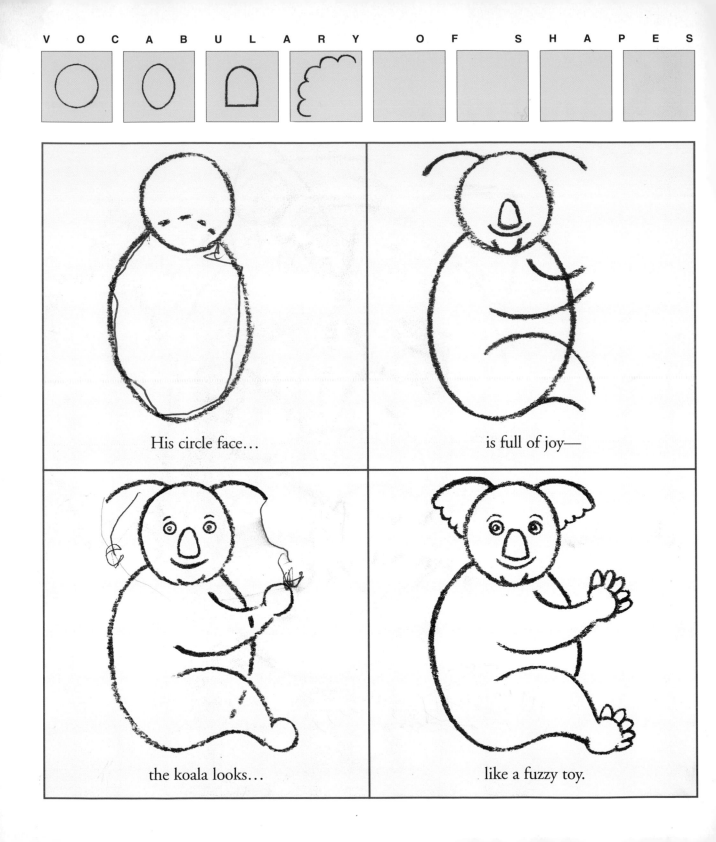

His circle face...

is full of joy—

the koala looks...

like a fuzzy toy.

Koala

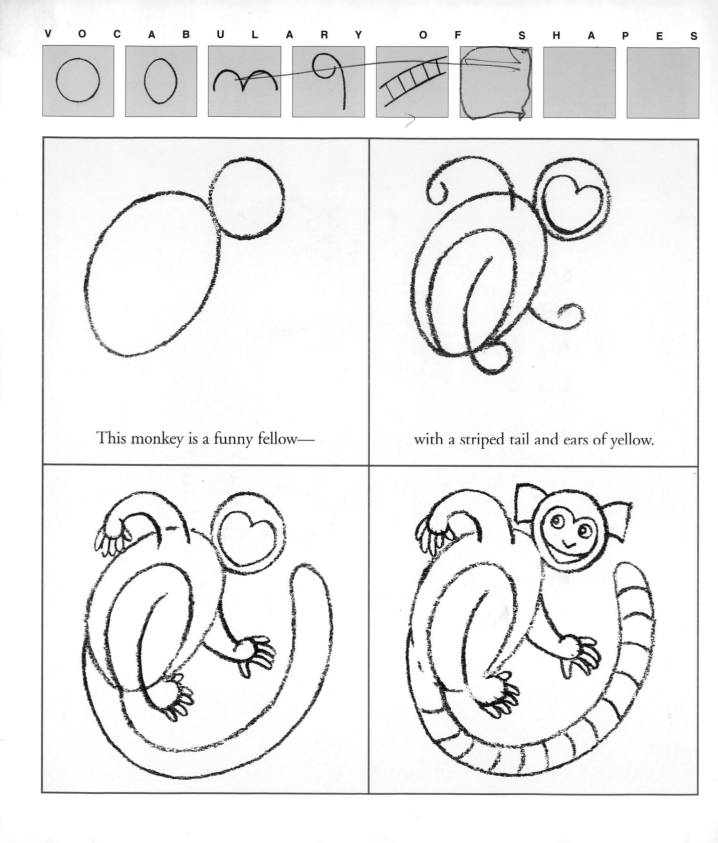

This monkey is a funny fellow—

with a striped tail and ears of yellow.

Marmoset

The camel, tiger, and bouncing kangaroo
are animals that share this planet with us, too.

Now that you've drawn them each from big to small,
you'll remember that the earth is home to us all.